BRENNAN MANNING

THE RAGAMUFFINGOSPEL

Visual Edition

MULTNOMAH PUBLISHERS, INC. · SISTERS, OREGON

All text in *The Ragamuffin Gospel Visual Edition* was taken
from the 2005 edition of *The Ragamuffin Gospel*
by Brennan Manning.

THE RAGAMUFFIN GOSPEL VISUAL EDITION
published by Multnomah Publishers, Inc.

The author is represented by Alive Communications, Inc.,
7680 Goddard St., Suite 200, Colorado Springs, CO 80920
© 2005 by Brennan Manning
International Standard Book Number: 1-59052-512-4

Cover and interior design by DesignWorks Group, Inc.
Charles Brock, designer/illustrator

Scripture quotations are from:
The New Jerusalem Bible
© 1985 by Darton, Longman & Todd, Ltd.
and Doubleday & Company, Inc.

Multnomah is a trademark of Multnomah Publishers, Inc.,
and is registered in the U.S. Patent and Trademark Office.
The colophon is a trademark of Multnomah Publishers, Inc.

Printed in China

For information:
MULTNOMAH PUBLISHERS, INC.
601 N. Larch St.
SISTERS, OREGON 97759

05 06 07 08 09 10—10 9 8 7 6 5 4 3 2 1 0

In the words of Francis of Assisi when he met Brother
Dominic on the road to Umbria..."Hi."

On my first reading of the book you're holding, I was
stretched. How dare the publisher include a mere 15
percent of my original manuscript! On the second
reading, I was stunned by the power of images to
expand and even transcend the power of words.
The Ragamuffin Gospel Visual Edition is a gem.
I pray that it touches you in the same way it has
touched me.

Under the mercy,

Brennan Manning

A Word Before

The Ragamuffin Gospel was written with a specific reading audience in mind.

This book is not for the superspiritual.

It is not for muscular Christians who have made John Wayne, and not Jesus, their hero.

It is not for academics who would imprison Jesus in the ivory tower of exegesis.

It is not for noisy, feel-good folks who manipulate Christianity into a naked appeal to emotion.

It is not for hooded mystics who want magic in their religion.

It is not for Alleluia Christians who live only on the mountaintop and have never visited the valley of desolation.

It is not for the fearless and tearless.

It is not for red-hot zealots who boast with the rich young ruler of the Gospels, "All these commandments I have kept from my youth."

It is not for the complacent who hoist over their shoulders a tote bag of honors, diplomas, and good works, actually believing they have it made.

It is not for legalists who would rather surrender control of their souls to rules than run the risk of living in union with Jesus.

If anyone is still reading along, *The Ragamuffin Gospel* was written for the bedraggled, beat-up, and burnt-out.

It is for the sorely burdened who are still shifting the heavy suitcase from one hand to the other.

It is for the wobbly and weak-kneed who know they don't have it all together and are too proud to accept the handout of amazing grace.

It is for inconsistent, unsteady disciples whose cheese is falling off their cracker.

It is for poor, weak, sinful men and women with hereditary faults and limited talents.

It is for earthen vessels who shuffle along on feet of clay.

It is for the bent and the bruised who feel that their lives are a grave disappointment to God.

It is for smart people who know they are stupid and honest disciples who admit they are scalawags.

The Ragamuffin Gospel is a book I wrote for myself and anyone who has grown weary and discouraged along the Way.

Brennan Manning

On a blustery October night in a church outside Minneapolis, several hundred believers had gathered for a three-day seminar. I began with a one-hour presentation on the gospel of grace and the reality of salvation. Using Scripture, story, symbolism, and personal experience, I focused on the total sufficiency of the redeeming work of Jesus Christ on Calvary. The service ended with a song and a prayer.

Leaving the church by a side door, the pastor turned to his associate and fumed, "Humph, that airhead didn't say one thing about what we have to do to earn our salvation!"

Something is radically wrong.

The bending of the mind by the powers of this world has twisted the gospel of grace into religious bondage and distorted the image of God into an eternal, small-minded bookkeeper. The Christian community resembles a Wall Street exchange of works wherein the elite are honored and the ordinary ignored. Love is stifled, freedom shackled, and self-righteousness fastened. The institutional church has become a wounder of the healers rather than a healer of the wounded.

Put bluntly, the American church today accepts grace in theory but denies it in practice. We say we believe that the fundamental structure of reality is grace, not works—but our lives refute our faith. By and large, the gospel of grace is neither proclaimed, understood, nor lived. Too many Christians are living in the house of fear and not in the house of love.

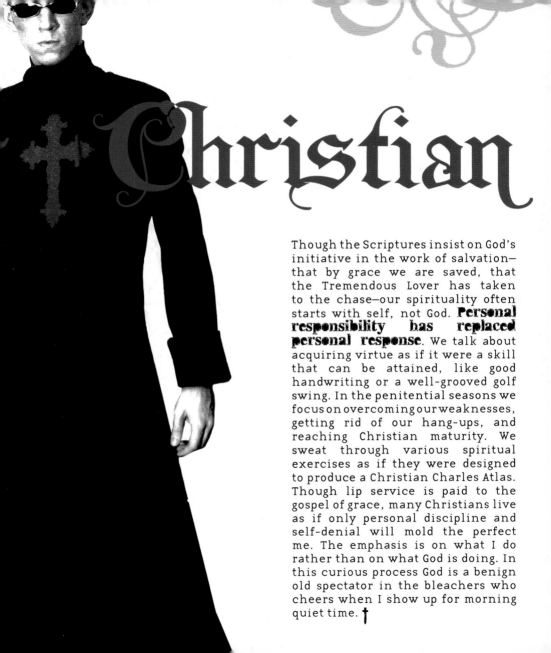

Christian

Though the Scriptures insist on God's initiative in the work of salvation—that by grace we are saved, that the Tremendous Lover has taken to the chase—our spirituality often starts with self, not God. **Personal responsibility has replaced personal response**. We talk about acquiring virtue as if it were a skill that can be attained, like good handwriting or a well-grooved golf swing. In the penitential seasons we focus on overcoming our weaknesses, getting rid of our hang-ups, and reaching Christian maturity. We sweat through various spiritual exercises as if they were designed to produce a Christian Charles Atlas. Though lip service is paid to the gospel of grace, many Christians live as if only personal discipline and self-denial will mold the perfect me. The emphasis is on what I do rather than on what God is doing. In this curious process God is a benign old spectator in the bleachers who cheers when I show up for morning quiet time. †

inadequacy
insufficie

WE BELIEVE THAT WE CAN PULL OURSELVES UP BY OUR
BOOTSTRAPS—INDEED, WE CAN DO IT OURSELVES.

SOONER OR LATER WE ARE CONFRONTED WITH THE PAINFUL
TRUTH OF OUR INADEQUACY AND INSUFFICIENCY. OUR SECURITY
IS SHATTERED AND OUR BOOTSTRAPS ARE CUT. ONCE THE FERVOR
HAS PASSED, WEAKNESS AND INFIDELITY APPEAR. WE DISCOVER
OUR INABILITY TO ADD EVEN A SINGLE INCH TO OUR SPIRITUAL
STATURE. THERE BEGINS A LONG WINTER OF DISCONTENT THAT
EVENTUALLY FLOWERS INTO GLOOM, PESSIMISM, AND A SUBTLE
DESPAIR—SUBTLE BECAUSE IT GOES UNRECOGNIZED, UNNOTICED,
AND THEREFORE UNCHALLENGED. IT TAKES THE FORM OF
BOREDOM, DRUDGERY. WE ARE OVERCOME BY THE
ORDINARINESS OF LIFE, BY DAILY DUTIES
DONE OVER AND OVER AGAIN.

SOMETHING IS RADICALLY WRON

Our huffing
and puffing to
impress God, our
scrambling for
brownie points,
our thrashing
about trying to
fix ourselves
while hiding
our pettiness
and wallowing
in guilt are
nauseating to
God and are a
flat denial of the
gospel of grace.

Our approach to
the Christian life
is as absurd as
the enthusiastic
young man who
had just received
his plumber's
license and was
taken to see
Niagara Falls. He
studied it for a
minute and then
said,

"I THINK I CAN FIX THIS."

SOMETHING IS
WRONG

I think I can fix it

I think I can't fix it

I think I can fix it

I think I can't fix it

I think I can fix it

I think I can't fix it

I think I can fix it

I think I can't fix it

I think I can fix it

I think I can't fix it

We secretly admit that the call of Jesus is too demanding, that surrender to the Spirit is beyond our reach. We start acting like everyone else. Life takes on a joyless, empty quality. We begin to resemble the leading character in Eugene O'Neill's play <u>The Great God Brown</u>: "Why am I afraid to dance, I who love music and rhythm and grace and song and laughter? Why am I afraid to live, I who love life and the beauty of flesh and the living colors of the earth and sky and sea? Why am I afraid to love, I who love love?"

why am I afraid to dance?

why am

I BELIEVE the Reformation
actually began the day Martin
Luther was praying over the
meaning of Paul's assertion
that the gospel reveals the
righteousness of God to us—it
shows how faith leads to faith
In other words, the RIGHTEOU
SHALL FIND LIFE THROUGH
FAITH (see Romans 1:17).
Like many Christians today,
Luther wrestled through th

night with
this core question: How could the gospel of
Christ be truly called "GOOD NEWS" if God
is a righteous judge who rewards the good and
punishes the evil? Did Jesus really have to
come to
reveal that
terrifying
message?

GOOD NEWS

How could
the

revelation of God in Christ Jesus be accurately
called "news" since the Old Testament carried
the same theme, or for that matter, "good" with
the threat of punishment hanging like a dark
cloud over the valley of history?

But as Jaroslav Pelikan notes:

Luther suddenly broke through
to the insight that the "righteousness of God"
that Paul spoke of in this passage was
not the righteousness by which God
was righteous in himself (that would
be passive righteousness) but the
righteousness by which, for the sake of
Jesus Christ, God made sinners righteous
(that is, active righteousness)
through the FORGIVENESS of sins in
justification. When he discovered that,
Luther said it was as though the very
Gates of Paradise had been opened to him.

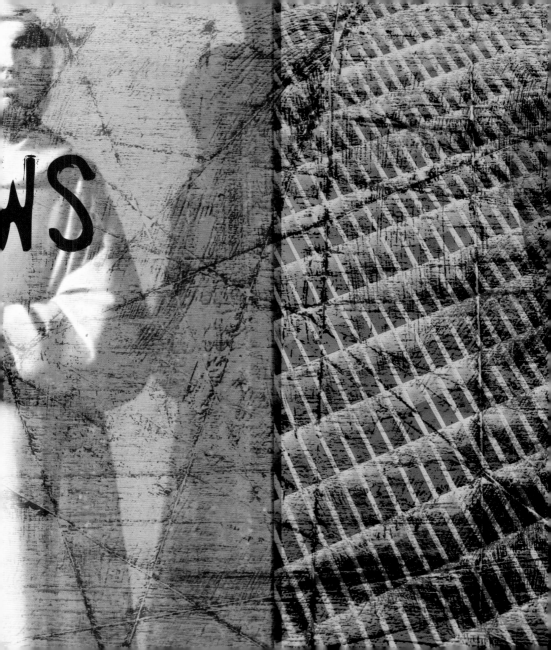

What a stunning truth!

"JUSTIFICATION BY GRACE THROUGH FAITH" is the theologian's learned phrase for what Chesterton once called "the furious love of God." He is not moody or capricious; He knows no seasons of change. He has a single relentless stance toward us: He loves us. He is the only God man has ever heard of who loves sinners. False gods—the gods of human manufacturing—despise sinners, but the Father of Jesus loves all, no matter what they do. But of course, this is almost too incredible for us to accept. Nevertheless, the central affirmation of the Reformation stands:

Gates of Paradise

Through no merit of ours, but by His mercy, we have been restored to a right relationship with God through the life, death, and resurrection of His beloved Son.

THIS IS THE GOOD NEWS, THE GOSPEL OF GRACE.

The word itself, "grace," has become trite and debased through misuse and overuse. It does not move us the way it moved our early Christian ancestors. In some European countries certain high ecclesiastical officials are still called "Your Grace." Sportswriters spoke of Michael Jordan's "easy grace," while business mogul Donald Trump has been described as "lacking in grace." A new perfume appears with "Grace" on the label, and a child's report card is called a "disgrace." The word has lost its raw, imaginative power.

Mercy is what pleases me, not sacrifice. And indeed I came to call not the upright, but sinners.

Matthew 9:9-13 captures a lovely glimpse of the gospel of grace: "As Jesus was walking on from there he saw a man named Matthew sitting at the tax office, and he said to him, 'Follow me.' And he got up and followed him. Now while he was at table in the house it happened that a number of tax collectors and sinners came to sit at the table with Jesus and his disciples. When the Pharisees saw this, they said to his disciples, 'Why does your master eat with tax collectors and sinners?' When he heard this he replied, 'It is not the healthy who need the doctor, but the sick. Go and learn the meaning of the words: Mercy is what pleases me, not sacrifice. And indeed I came to call not the upright, but sinners.'"

Here is revelation bright as the evening star: Jesus comes for sinners, for those as outcast as tax collectors and for those caught up in squalid choices and failed dreams. He comes for corporate executives, street people, superstars, farmers, hookers, addicts, IRS agents, AIDS victims, and even used-car salesmen. Jesus not only talks with these people but dines with them—fully aware that His table fellowship with sinners will raise the eyebrows of religious bureaucrats who hold up the robes and insignia of their authority to justify their condemnation of the truth and their rejection of the gospel of grace.

Every Christian generation tries to dim the blinding brightness of its meaning because the gospel seems too good to be true.

Jesus says the kingdom of His Father is not a subdivision for the self-righteous nor for those who feel they possess the state secret of salvation. The kingdom is not an exclusive, well-trimmed suburb with snobbish rules about who can live there. No, it is for a larger, homelier, less self-conscious caste of people who understand they are sinners because they have experienced the yaw and pitch of moral struggle.

These are the sinner-guests invited by Jesus to closeness with Him around the banquet table. It remains a startling story to those who never understand that the men and women who are truly filled with light are those who have gazed deeply into the darkness of their imperfect existence. Perhaps it was after meditating on this passage that Morton Kelsey wrote, "The church is not a museum for saints but a hospital for sinners."

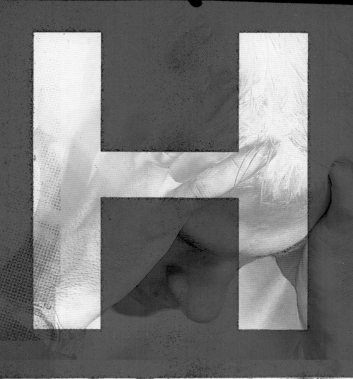

The Good News means we can stop lying to ourselves. The sweet sound of amazing grace saves us from the necessity of self-deception. It keeps us from denying that though Christ was victorious, the battle with lust, greed, and pride still rages within us. As a sinner who has been redeemed, I can acknowledge that I am often unloving, irritable, angry, and resentful with those closest to me. When I go to church I can leave my white hat at home and admit I have failed. God not only loves me as I am, but also knows me as I am. Because of this I don't need to apply spiritual cosmetics to make myself presentable to Him. I can accept ownership of my poverty and powerlessness and neediness.

When I get honest, I admit I am a bundle of paradoxes. I believe and I doubt, I hope and get discouraged, I love and I hate, I feel bad about feeling good, I feel guilty about not feeling guilty. I am trusting and suspicious. I am honest and I still play games. Aristotle said I am a rational animal;

BUNDLE OF

I say I am an angel with an incredible capacity for beer.

To live by grace means to acknowledge my whole life story, the light side and the dark. In admitting my shadow side, I learn who I am and what God's grace means. As Thomas Merton put it, **A saint is not someone who is good but who experiences the goodness of God**.

The gospel of grace nullifies our adulation of televangelists, charismatic superstars, and local church heroes. It obliterates the two-class citizenship theory operative in many American churches. For grace proclaims the awesome truth that all is gift. All that is good is ours, not by right, but by the sheer bounty of a gracious God. While there is much we may have earned—our degree, our

PARADOXES

salary, our home and garden, a Miller Lite, and a good night's sleep—all this is possible only because we have been given so much: life itself, eyes to see and hands to touch, a mind to shape ideas, and a heart to beat with love. We have been given God in our souls and Christ in our flesh. We have the power to believe where others deny, to hope where others despair, to love where others hurt. This and so much more is sheer gift; it is not reward for our faithfulness, our generous disposition, or our heroic life of prayer. Even our fidelity is a gift. "If we but turn to God," said St. Augustine, "that itself is a gift of God."

My deepest awareness of myself is that **I am deeply loved by Jesus Christ and I have done nothing to earn it or deserve it.**

The Good News of the gospel of grace cries out: We are all, equally, privileged but unentitled beggars at the door of God's mercy! In Luke 18, a rich young man comes to Jesus, asking what he must do to inherit eternal life. He wants to be in the spotlight. It is no coincidence that Luke juxtaposes the passage of Jesus and the children immediately preceding the verses on the young aristocrat. Children contrast with the rich man simply because there is no question of their having yet been able to merit anything. Jesus' point is, there is nothing that any of us can do to inherit the kingdom. We must simply receive it like little children. And little children haven't done anything. The New Testament world was not sentimental about children and had no illusion about any pretended innate goodness in them. Jesus is not suggesting that heaven is a huge playground for Cajun infants. Children are our model because they have no claim on heaven. If they are close to God, it is because they are incompetent, not because they are innocent. If they receive anything, it can only be as a gift.

Paul writes in Ephesians, "Because it is by grace that you have been saved, through faith; not by anything of your own, but by a gift from God; not by anything that you have done, so that nobody can claim the credit" (2:8-9). †

YOU ARE ACCEPTED

YOU ARE ACCEPTED

"Grace strikes us when we are in great pain and restlessness. It strikes us when we walk through the dark valley of a meaningless and empty life... It strikes us when, year after year, the longed-for perfection does not appear, when the old compulsions reign within us as they have for decades, when despair destroys all joy and courage. Sometimes at that moment a wave of light breaks into our darkness, and it is as though a voice were saying: 'You are accepted. You are accepted, accepted by that which is greater than you, and the name of which you do not know. Do not ask for the name now; perhaps you will find it later. Do not try to do anything now; perhaps later you will do much. Do not seek for anything, do not perform anything, do not intend anything. Simply accept the fact that you are accepted.' If that happens to us, we experience grace" (Paul Tillich).

Grace calls out, "You are not just a disillusioned old man who may die soon, a middle-aged woman stuck in a job and desperately wanting to get out, a young person feeling the fire in the belly begin to grow cold. You may be insecure, inadequate, mistaken, or potbellied. Death, panic, depression, and disillusionment may be near you. But you are not just that. You are accepted."

Never confuse your perception of yourself with the mystery that you really are accepted.

grace in kindness toward...
Jesus. [8]For by grace you have...
saved [a]through faith. And [b]this...
[c]our own doing; [d]it is the [e]gift of...
...of works, [f]so that...

My grace is

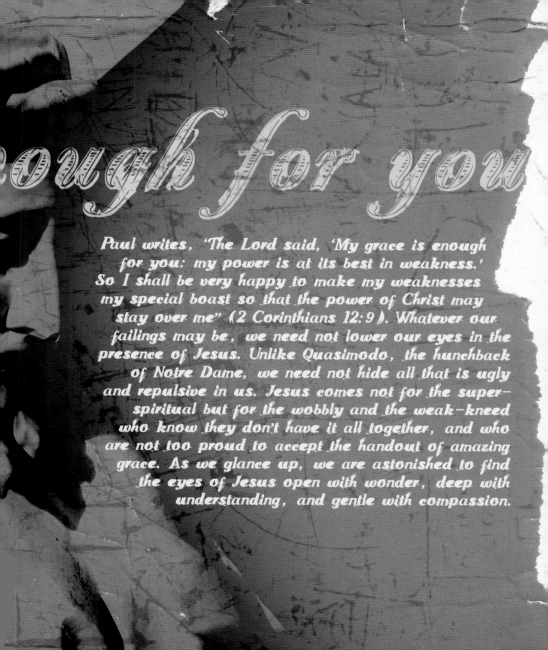

ough for you

Paul writes, "The Lord said, 'My grace is enough for you: my power is at its best in weakness.' So I shall be very happy to make my weaknesses my special boast so that the power of Christ may stay over me" (2 Corinthians 12:9). Whatever our failings may be, we need not lower our eyes in the presence of Jesus. Unlike Quasimodo, the hunchback of Notre Dame, we need not hide all that is ugly and repulsive in us. Jesus comes not for the super-spiritual but for the wobbly and the weak-kneed who know they don't have it all together, and who are not too proud to accept the handout of amazing grace. As we glance up, we are astonished to find the eyes of Jesus open with wonder, deep with understanding, and gentle with compassion.

How I treat a brother or sister from day to day, how I react to the sin-scarred wino on the street, how I respond to interruptions from people I dislike, how I deal with normal people in their normal confusion on a normal day may be a better indication of my reverence for life than the antiabortion sticker on the bumper of my car.

We are not pro-life simply because we are warding off death. We are pro-life to the extent that we are men and women for others, all others; to the extent that no human flesh is a stranger to us; to the extent that we can touch the hand of another in love; to the extent that for us there are no "others."

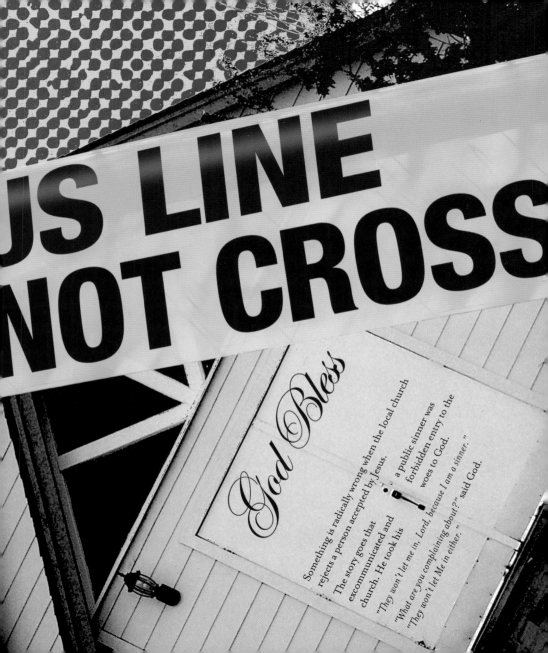

JS LINE
NOT CROSS

God Bless

Something is radically wrong when the local church rejects a person accepted by Jesus.

The story goes that a public sinner was excommunicated and forbidden entry to the church. He took his woes to God.

"They won't let me in, Lord, because I am a sinner."

"What are you complaining about?" said God. "They won't let Me in either."

There is a myth flourishing in the church today that has caused incalculable harm: once converted, fully convertead. In other words, once I accept Jesus Christ as my Lord and Savior, an irreversible, sinless future beckons. Discipleship will be an untarnished success story; life will be an unbroken upward spiral toward holiness. Tell that to poor Peter who, after three times professing his love for Jesus on the beach and after receiving the fullness of the Spirit at Pentecost, was still jealous of Paul's apostolic success.

Often I have been asked, "Brennan, how is it possible that you became an alcoholic after you got saved?" It is possible because I got battered and bruised by loneliness and failure; because I got discouraged, uncertain, guilt-ridden, and took my eyes off Jesus. Because **the Christ-encounter did not transfigure me into an angel**. Because justification by grace through faith means I have been set in right relationship with God, not made the equivalent of a patient etherized on a table. †

battered

bruised

AGAIN

discouraged

uncertain

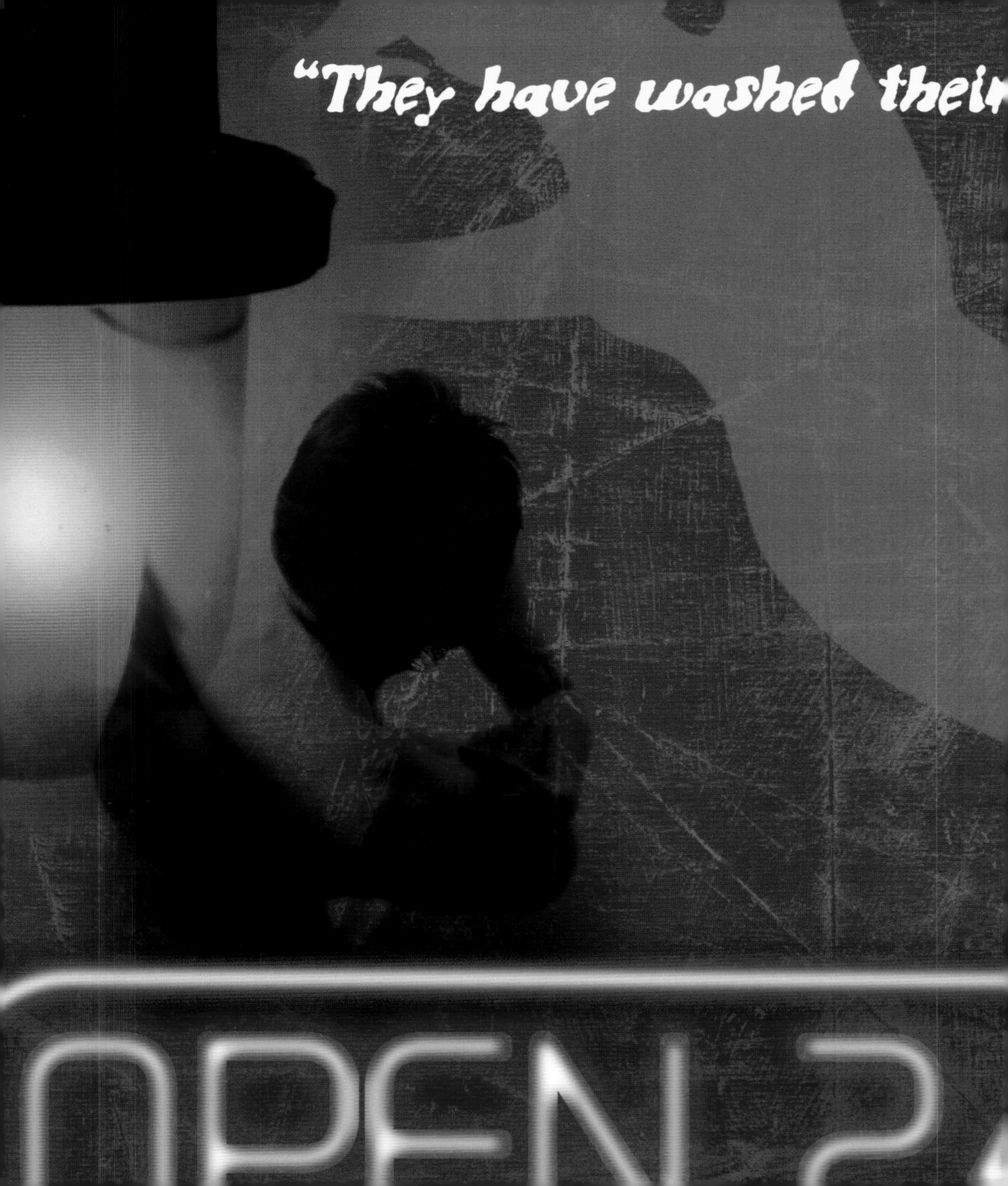

“They have washed thei
OPEN 2

robes and made them white in the blood of the Lamb."

Because salvation is by grace through faith, I believe that among the countless number of people standing in front of the throne and in front of the Lamb, dressed in white robes and holding palms in their hands (see Revelation 7:9), I shall see the prostitute from the Kit-Kat Ranch in Carson City, Nevada, who tearfully told me she could find no other employment to support her two-year-old son. I shall see the woman who had an abortion and is haunted by guilt and remorse but did the best she could faced with grueling alternatives; the businessman besieged with debt who sold his integrity in a series of desperate transactions; the insecure clergyman addicted to being liked, who never challenged his people from the pulpit and longed for unconditional love; the sexually abused teen molested by his father and now selling his body on the street, who, as he falls asleep each night after his last "trick," whispers the name of the unknown God he learned about in Sunday school; the deathbed convert who for decades had his cake and ate it, broke every law of God and man, wallowed in lust, and raped the earth.

"But how?" we ask.

Then the voice says, "They have washed their robes and made them white in the blood of the Lamb."

There they are. There we are—the multitude who so wanted to be faithful, who at times got defeated, soiled by life, and bested by trials, wearing the bloodied garments of life's tribulations, but through it all clung to the faith.

My friends, if this is not good news to you, you have never understood the gospel of grace.

HOURS

if that is not good news to you, you have never understood the gospel of grace

ORDER

Sir James Jeans, the famous British astronomer, once said, "The universe appears to have been designed by a Pure Mathematician." Joseph Campbell wrote of "a perception of a cosmic order, mathematically definable."

The slant of the earth, for example, tilted at an angle of twenty-three degrees, produces our seasons. Scientists tell us that if the earth had not been tilted exactly as it is, vapors from the oceans would move both north and south, piling up vast continents of ice.

23°

If the moon were only 50,000 miles away from earth instead of 250,000, the tides might be so enormous that all continents would be submerged in water—even the mountains would be eroded.

If the crust of the earth had been only ten feet thicker, there would be no oxygen, and without it all animal life would die.

Had the oceans been a few feet deeper, carbon dioxide and oxygen would have been absorbed and no vegetable life would exist.

THE EARTH'S WEIGHT HAS BEEN ESTIMATED AT SIX SEXTILLION TONS (THAT'S A SIX WITH TWENTY-ONE ZEROS). YET IT IS PERFECTLY BALANCED AND TURNS EASILY ON ITS AXIS. IT ROTATES DAILY AT THE RATE OF MORE THAN A THOUSAND MILES PER HOUR, OR 25,000 MILES EACH DAY. THIS ADDS UP TO NINE MILLION MILES A YEAR. CONSIDERING THE TREMENDOUS WEIGHT OF SIX SEXTILLION TONS ROLLING AT THIS FANTASTIC SPEED AROUND AN INVISIBLE AXIS, HELD IN PLACE BY UNSEEN BANDS OF GRAVITATION, THE WORDS OF JOB 26:7 TAKE ON UNPARALLELED SIGNIFICANCE: "HE POISED THE EARTH ON NOTHINGNESS."

THINK BIG

ABOUT

GOD

The nine major planets in our solar system range in distance from the sun from 36 million to about 3,664 million miles; yet each moves around the sun in exact precision, with orbits ranging from 88 days for Mercury to 248 years for Pluto.

Still, the sun is only one minor star among the 100 billion burning orbs that comprise our Milky Way galaxy. If you were to hold out a dime at arm's length while gazing at the night sky, the coin would block out 15 million stars from your view, if your eyes could see with that power.

When we attempt to comprehend the almost countless stars and other heavenly bodies in our galaxy alone, we resonate to Isaiah's paean of praise to the all-powerful Creator: "Lift your eyes and look: he who created these things leads out their army in order, summoning each of them by name. **So mighty is his power, so great his strength**, that not one fails to answer" (40:26).

Creation discloses a power that baffles our minds and beggars our speech. We are enamored and enchanted by God's power. We **stutter and stammer** about God's holiness. We tremble before God's majesty and yet...we grow squeamish and skittish before God's love. †

In my ministry as a vagabond evangelist, I have encountered shocking resistance to the God whom the Bible defines as Love. The skeptics range from the oily, over-polite professionals who discreetly drop hints of the heresy of universalism, to the Bible thumper who sees only the dusty, robust war God of the Pentateuch, and who insists on restating the cold demands of rule-ridden perfectionism.

Our resistance to the furious love of God may be traced to the church, our parents and pastors, and life itself. Yet if we were truly men and women of prayer, our faces set like flint and our hearts laid waste by passion, we would discard our excuses. We must go out into a

desert of some kind (your backyard will do) and come into a personal experience of the awesome love of God...the God of the gospel of grace. A God who, out of love for us, sent the only Son He ever had wrapped in our skin. He learned how to walk, stumbled and fell, cried for His milk, sweated blood in the night, was lashed with a whip and showered with spit, was fixed to a cross, and died whispering forgiveness on us all.

Yes, the gracious God enfleshed in Jesus Christ loves us. And grace is the active expression of His love.

The gospel of grace ends any apparent dichotomy between God's power and His love. For the work of creating is an act of love.

The God who flung from His fingertips this universe filled with galaxies and stars, penguins and puffins, gulls and gannets, Pomeranians and poodles, elephants and evergreens, parrots and potato bugs, peaches and pears, and a world full of children made in His own image, is the God who loves with magnificent monotony.

He has gone to stay

at a sinner's house

After reading the entire Gospel of Luke for the first time, a post-Valley girl said: "**Wow**! **Like Jesus has this totally intense thing for ragamuffins**."

The young lady is onto something.

Jesus spent a disproportionate amount of time with people described in the Gospels as the poor, the blind, the lame, the lepers, the hungry, sinners, prostitutes, tax collectors, the persecuted, the downtrodden, the captives, those possessed by unclean spirits, all who labor and are heavy burdened, the rabble who know nothing of the law, the crowds, the little ones, the least, the last, and the lost sheep of the house of Israel.

In short, Jesus hung out with ragamuffins. Obviously His love for failures and nobodies was not an exclusive love—that would merely substitute one class prejudice for another. But one of the mysteries of the gospel tradition is this strange attraction of Jesus for the unattractive, this strange desire for the undesirable, this strange love for the unlovely. The key to this mystery is, of course, Abba. Jesus does what He sees the Father doing; He loves those whom the Father loves.

It did not escape the Pharisees' attention that Jesus meant to befriend the rabble. He was not only breaking the law, He was destroying the very structure of Jewish society. "They all complained when they saw what was happening. 'He has gone to stay at a sinner's house,' they said" (Luke 19:7). But Zacchaeus, not too hung up on respectability, was overwhelmed with joy. †

The sinners to whom Jesus directed His messianic ministry were not those who skipped morning devotions or Sunday church. His ministry was to those whom society considered real sinners. They had done nothing to merit salvation, yet they opened themselves to the gift that was offered them.

Through table fellowship Jesus ritually acted out His insight into Abba's indiscriminate love.

I GOT DRUNK

AND STAYED DRUNK

FOR FIVE DAYS

On a sweltering summer night in New Orleans, sixteen recovering alcoholics and drug addicts gather for their weekly AA meeting. Although several members attend other meetings during the week, this is their home group. They have been meeting on Tuesday nights for several years and know each other well. Some talk to each other daily on the telephone; others socialize outside the meetings. The personal investment in one another's sobriety is sizable. Nobody fools anybody else. Everyone is there because he or she made a slobbering mess of his or her life and is trying to put the pieces back together. Each meeting is marked by levity and seriousness. Some members are wealthy, others middle class or poor. Some smoke, others don't. Most drink coffee. Some have graduate degrees, others have not finished high school. For one small hour, the high and the mighty descend and the lowly rise. The result is fellowship.

The meeting opened with the Serenity Prayer followed by a moment of silence. The prologue to Alcoholics Anonymous was read from the Big Book by Harry, followed by the Twelve Steps of the program from Michelle. That night, Jack was the appointed leader. "The theme I would like to talk about tonight is gratitude," he began, "but if anyone wants to talk about something else, let's hear it."

Immediately Phil's hand shot up.

"As you all know, last week I went up to Pennsylvania to visit family and missed the meeting. You also know I have been sober for seven years. Last Monday **I got drunk and stayed drunk** for five days."

The only sound in the room was the drip of Mr. Coffee in the corner.

"You all know the buzz word, H.A.L.T., in this program," he continued. "Don't let yourself get hungry, angry, lonely, or tired or you will be very vulnerable for the first drink. The last three got to me. I unplugged the jug and…"

Phil's voice choked and he lowered his head. I glanced around the table— moist eyes, tears of compassion, soft sobbing the only sound in the room.

"The same thing happened to me, Phil, but I stayed drunk for a year."

"Thank God you're back."

"Boy, that took a lot of guts."

"**Relapse spells relief**, Phil," said a substance abuse counselor.

"Let's get together tomorrow and figure out what you needed relief from and why."

"I'm so proud of you."

"Hell, I never made even close to seven years."

As the meeting ended, Phil stood up. He felt a hand on his shoulder, another on his face. Then kisses on his eyes, forehead, neck, and cheek. "**You old ragamuffin**," said Denise. "Let's go. I'm treating you to a banana split at Tastee Freeze." †

You old
ragamuffin

AS HE SETS THE CHILD ON HIS KNEE

The ragamuffin gospel reveals that Jesus forgives sins, including sins of the flesh; that He is comfortable with sinners who remember how to show compassion; but that He cannot and will not have a relationship with pretenders in the Spirit.

In His reply to the disciples' question about who is the greatest in the kingdom of heaven, He said, "So he called a little child to him whom he set among them. Then he said, 'In truth I tell you, unless you change and become like little children **you will never enter the kingdom of Heaven**. And so, the one who makes himself as little as this little child is the greatest in the kingdom of Heaven'" (Matthew 18:2–4).

As He sets the child on His knee, Jesus cuts to the heart of the matter. A child is unself-conscious, incapable of pretense.

I am reminded of the night little John Dyer, three years old, knocked on our door flanked by his parents. I looked down and said, "Hi, John. I am delighted to see you." He looked neither to the right nor left. His face was set like flint. He narrowed his eyes with the apocalyptic glint of an aimed gun. "**Where's the cookies?**" he demanded. †

A CHILD IS UNSELF
OF PRETENSE...
HE NARROWED HIS EYES
GLINT OF AN AIMED

"WHERE'S

conscious, incapable

with the apocalyptic

gun.

THE COOKIES?"

HE DEMANDED.

The lowest and the least

We tend to idealize childhood as the happy age of innocence, insouciance, and simple faith; but in New Testament times the child was considered of no importance, meriting little attention or favor. According to Albert Nolan, "Children in that society had no status at all—they did not count." The child was regarded with scorn.

For the disciple of Jesus, "becoming like a little child" means the willingness to accept oneself as being of little account and to be regarded as unimportant. The little child who is the image of the kingdom is a symbol of those who have the lowest places in society, the poor and the oppressed, the beggars, the prostitutes and tax collectors—the people whom Jesus often called the "little ones" or the "least." Jesus' concern was that these little ones should not be despised or treated as inferior (see Matthew 18:10). He was well aware of their feelings of shame and inferiority, and because of His compassion they were, in His eyes, of extraordinarily great value. As far as He was concerned, they had nothing to fear. The kingdom was theirs. **"There is no need to be afraid**, little flock, for it has pleased your Father to give you the kingdom" (Luke 12:32).

Jesus gave these scorned little ones a privileged place in the kingdom and presented them as models to would-be disciples. They were to accept the kingdom in the same way a child would accept her allowance. If the children were privileged, it was not because they had merited privilege, but simply because God took pleasure in these little ones whom adults despised.

There is a wondrous open-mindedness about children and an insatiable desire to learn from life. An open attitude is like an open door—a welcoming disposition toward the fellow travelers who knock on our door during the middle of a day, the middle of the week, or the middle of a lifetime.

If we maintain the open-mindedness of children, we challenge fixed ideas and established structures, including our own. We listen to people in other denominations and religions. We don't find demons in those with whom we disagree. We don't cozy up to people who mouth our jargon. We focus on both/and, fully aware that God's truth cannot be imprisoned in a small definition. †

A man walked into the doctor's office and said, "Doctor, I have this awful headache that never leaves me. Could you give me something for it?"

"I will," said the doctor, "but I want to check a few things out first. Tell me, do you drink a lot of liquor?"

"Liquor?" said the man indignantly. "I never touch the filthy stuff."

"How about smoking?"

"I think smoking is disgusting. I've never in my life touched tobacco."

"I'm a bit embarrassed to ask this, but—you know the way some men are—do you do any running around at night?"

"Of course not. What do you take me for? I'm in bed every night by ten o'clock at the latest."

"Tell me," said the doctor, "the pain in the head you speak of, is it a sharp, shooting kind of pain?"

"Yes," said the man. "That's it—a sharp, shooting kind of pain."

"Simple, my dear fellow! Your trouble is you have your halo on too tight. All we need to do is loosen it a bit."

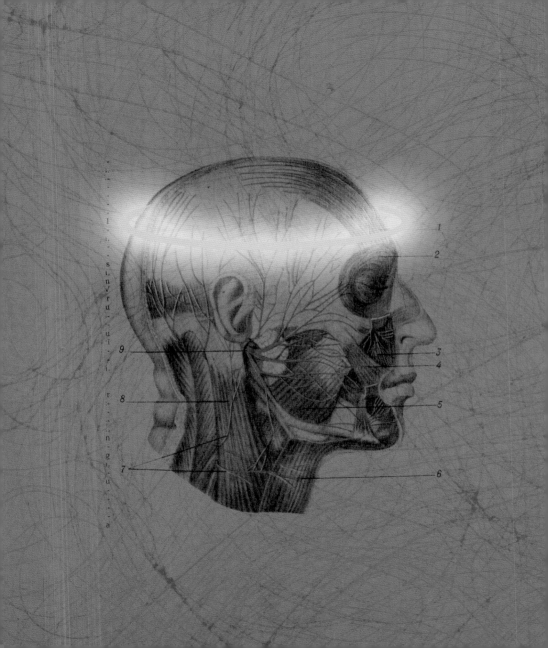

CAUTION!
HALO TOO TIGHT

Trapped in the fatal narcis

The kingdom belongs to people who aren't trying to look good or impress anybody, even themselves. They are not plotting how they can call attention to themselves, worrying about how their actions will be interpreted or wondering if they will get gold stars for their behavior. Twenty centuries later, Jesus speaks pointedly to the preening ascetic trapped in the fatal narcissism of spiritual perfectionism, to those of us caught up in boasting about our victories in the vineyard, to those of us fretting and flapping about our human weaknesses and character defects. The child doesn't have to struggle to get himself in a good position for having a relationship with God; he doesn't have to craft ingenious ways of explaining his position to Jesus; he doesn't have to create a pretty face for himself; he doesn't have to achieve any state of spiritual feeling or intellectual understanding. All he has to do is happily **accept the cookies**, the gift of the kingdom. †

3m of spiritual perfectionism

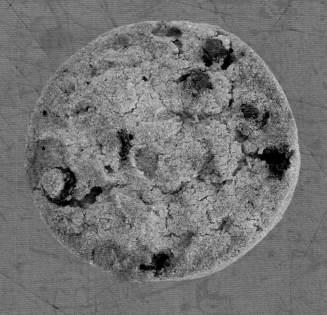

Accept the Cookies

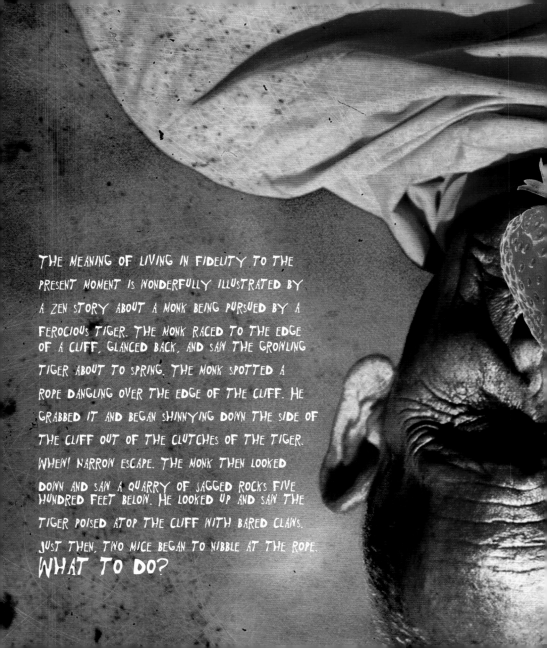

THE MEANING OF LIVING IN FIDELITY TO THE PRESENT MOMENT IS WONDERFULLY ILLUSTRATED BY A ZEN STORY ABOUT A MONK BEING PURSUED BY A FEROCIOUS TIGER. THE MONK RACED TO THE EDGE OF A CLIFF, GLANCED BACK, AND SAW THE GROWLING TIGER ABOUT TO SPRING. THE MONK SPOTTED A ROPE DANGLING OVER THE EDGE OF THE CLIFF. HE GRABBED IT AND BEGAN SHINNYING DOWN THE SIDE OF THE CLIFF OUT OF THE CLUTCHES OF THE TIGER. WHEW! NARROW ESCAPE. THE MONK THEN LOOKED DOWN AND SAW A QUARRY OF JAGGED ROCKS FIVE HUNDRED FEET BELOW. HE LOOKED UP AND SAW THE TIGER POISED ATOP THE CLIFF WITH BARED CLAWS. JUST THEN, TWO MICE BEGAN TO NIBBLE AT THE ROPE.

WHAT TO DO?

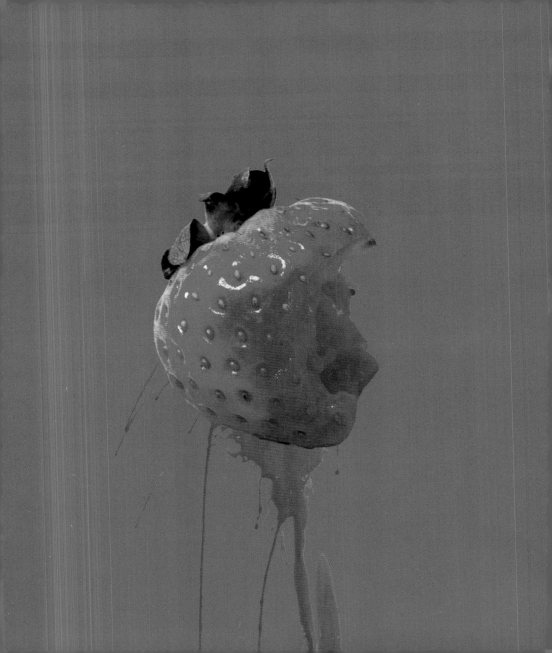

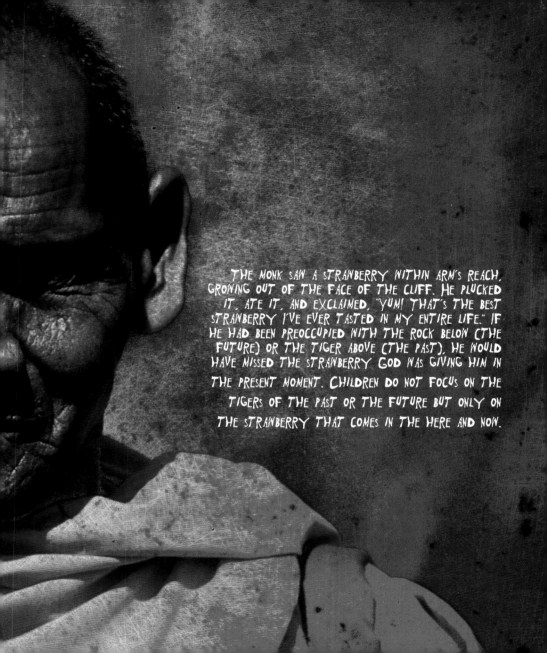

THE MONK SAW A STRANBERRY WITHIN ARM'S REACH, GROWING OUT OF THE FACE OF THE CLIFF. HE PLUCKED IT, ATE IT, AND EXCLAIMED, "YUM! THAT'S THE BEST STRANBERRY I'VE EVER TASTED IN MY ENTIRE LIFE." IF HE HAD BEEN PREOCCUPIED WITH THE ROCK BELOW (THE FUTURE) OR THE TIGER ABOVE (THE PAST), HE WOULD HAVE MISSED THE STRANBERRY GOD WAS GIVING HIM IN THE PRESENT MOMENT. CHILDREN DO NOT FOCUS ON THE TIGERS OF THE PAST OR THE FUTURE BUT ONLY ON THE STRANBERRY THAT COMES IN THE HERE AND NOW.

The tilted halo of the saved sinner is worn loosely and with easy grace. We have discovered that the cross accomplished far more than revealing the love of God. The blood of the Lamb points to the truth of grace: what we cannot do for ourselves, God has done for us. On the cross, somehow, someway, Christ bore our sins, took our place, and died for us. At the cross, Jesus unmasks the sinner not only as a beggar but as a criminal before God. Jesus Christ bore our sins and bore them away. We cannot wash away the stain of our sins, but He is the Lamb who has taken away the sins of the world.

The sinner saved by grace is haunted by Calvary, by the cross, and especially by the question, **Why did He die?** A clue comes from the Gospel of John: "For this is how God loved the world: he gave his only Son, so that everyone who believes in him may not perish but may have eternal life." Another clue from Paul's cry in Galatians: "**He loved me** and delivered himself up for me." The answer lies in love.

One thing we do know: We don't comprehend the love of Jesus Christ.

Oh, we see a movie and resonate to what a young man and woman will endure for romantic love. We know that when the chips are down, if we love wildly enough we'll fling life and caution to the winds for the one we love. But when it comes to God's love in the broken, blood-drenched body of Jesus Christ, we get antsy and start to talk about theology, divine justice, God's wrath, and the heresy of universalism.

The saved sinner is prostrate in adoration, lost in wonder and praise. He knows repentance is not what we do in order to earn forgiveness; it is what we do because we have been forgiven. It serves as an expression of gratitude rather than an effort to earn forgiveness. Thus the sequence of forgiveness and then repentance, rather than repentance and then forgiveness, is crucial for understanding the gospel of grace.

For many, God sits up there like a Buddha, impassive, unmoving, hard as flint. Calvary cries out more clearly than any theology textbook: We do not know our God. We have not grasped the truth in the First Letter of John: "In this is love, not that we loved God but that He loved us and sent His Son to be the propitiation for our sins." The cross reveals the depth of the Father's love for us: "For greater love than this no one has than that he lay down his life for his friends."

Why? ➡

Haunted by the cross

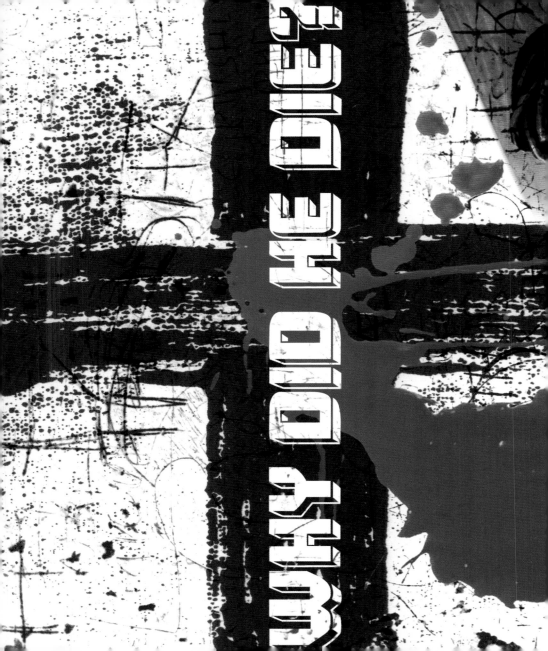

Because we never lay hold of our nothingness before God, and consequently, we never enter into the deepest reality of our relationship with Him. But when we accept ownership of our powerlessness and helplessness, when we acknowledge that we are paupers at the door of God's mercy, then God can make something beautiful out of us. †

WE ARE PALPERS AT THE| DOOR| OF GODs MERCY

God can make something
beautiful out of us

I BROUGHT MYSELF

Should you ask the biblically poor woman to describe her prayer life, she might answer, "Most of the time, my prayer consists in experiencing the absence of God in the hope of communion." She is not richly endowed with mystical experiences. That is fine because it reflects the truth of her impoverished humanity.

Yet the experience of absence does not mean the absence of experience. For example, the soldier in combat who, during a lull in the battle, steals a glance at his wife's picture tucked in his helmet, is more present to her at that moment in her absence than he is to the rifle that is present in his hands. Likewise, the poor in spirit perceive that religious experience and mystical "highs" are not the goal of authentic prayer; rather, the goal is communion with God.

The Christian who is truly poor in spirit goes to worship on Sunday morning singing, "I am poor but I brought myself the best I could. I am Yours, I am Yours."

THE BEST I COULD

When a man or woman is truly honest (not just working at it) it is virtually impossible to insult them personally. There is nothing there to insult. Those who were truly ready for the kingdom were just such people. Their inner poverty of spirit and rigorous honesty had set them free. They were people who had nothing to be proud of.

There was the sinful woman in the village who kissed Jesus' feet. There was freedom in doing that. Despised as a prostitute, she had accepted the truth of her utter nothingness before the Lord. She had nothing to lose. She loved much because much had been forgiven her.

We have to be converted

from the bad news

The disciple living by grace rather than law has undergone a decisive conversion—a turning from mistrust to trust. The foremost characteristic of living by grace is trust in the redeeming work of Jesus Christ.

To believe deeply, as Jesus did, that God is present and at work in human life is to understand that I am a beloved child of this Father and, hence, free to trust. That makes a profound difference in the way I relate to myself and others; it makes an enormous difference in the way I live. To trust Abba, both in prayer and life, is to stand in childlike openness before a mystery of gracious love and acceptance.

The tendency in legalistic religion is to mistrust God, to mistrust others, and consequently, to mistrust ourselves.

Do you really believe that the Father of our Lord and Savior Jesus Christ is gracious, that He cares about you? Do you really believe that He is always, unfailingly present to you as companion and support? **Do you really believe that God is love?**

Or have you learned to fear this loving and gracious Father? "In love," John says, "there is no room for fear, but perfect love drives out fear, because fear implies punishment and no one who is afraid has come to perfection in love" (1 John 4:18). Have you learned to think of the Father as the judge, the spy, the disciplinarian, the punisher? If you think that way, you are wrong.

Abba is not our enemy. If we think that, we are wrong.

Abba is not intent on trying and tempting and testing us. If we think that, we are wrong.

Abba does not prefer and promote suffering and pain. If we think that, we are wrong.

Jesus brings good news about the Father, not bad news. "The time is fulfilled," Jesus said, "and the kingdom of God is close at hand. **Repent, and believe the gospel**" (Mark 1:15). We have to be converted from the bad news to the good news, from expecting nothing to expecting something.

Trust defines the meaning of living by grace rather than works. Trust is like climbing a fifty-foot ladder, reaching the top, and hearing someone down below yell, "Jump!" The trusting disciple has this childlike confidence in a loving Father. Trust says, in effect, "Abba, just on the basis of what You have shown me in Your Son, Jesus, I believe You love me. You have forgiven me. You will hold me and never let me go. Therefore, **I trust You with my life.**" †

If a random sampling of one thousand American Christians were taken today,
earlier times it did not take faith to believe that God existed—almost
relationship to God—whether one trusted in God. The difference between fai
"trusting in God" is enormous. The first is a matter of the head, the seco
intrinsically brings change.

THE MAJORITY WOULD DEFINE FAITH AS BELIEF IN THE EXISTENCE OF GOD. IN

EVERYBODY TOOK THAT FOR GRANTED. RATHER, FAITH HAD TO DO WITH ONE'S

AS "BELIEF IN SOMETHING THAT MAY OR MAY NOT EXIST" AND FAITH AS

A MATTER OF THE HEART. THE FIRST CAN LEAVE US UNCHANGED; THE SECOND

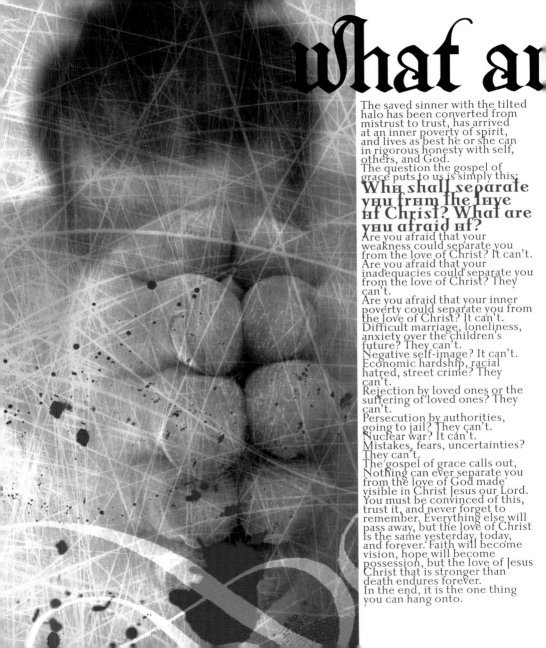

The saved sinner with the tilted halo has been converted from mistrust to trust, has arrived at an inner poverty of spirit, and lives as best he or she can in rigorous honesty with self, others, and God.

The question the gospel of grace puts to us is simply this:

Who shall separate you from the love of Christ? What are you afraid of?

Are you afraid that your weakness could separate you from the love of Christ? It can't.

Are you afraid that your inadequacies could separate you from the love of Christ? They can't.

Are you afraid that your inner poverty could separate you from the love of Christ? It can't.

Difficult marriage, loneliness, anxiety over the children's future? They can't.

Negative self-image? It can't.

Economic hardship, racial hatred, street crime? They can't.

Rejection by loved ones or the suffering of loved ones? They can't.

Persecution by authorities, going to jail? They can't.

Nuclear war? It can't.

Mistakes, fears, uncertainties? They can't.

The gospel of grace calls out, Nothing can ever separate you from the love of God made visible in Christ Jesus our Lord. You must be convinced of this, trust it, and never forget to remember. Everything else will pass away, but the love of Christ is the same yesterday, today, and forever. Faith will become vision, hope will become possession, but the love of Jesus Christ that is stronger than death endures forever.

In the end, it is the one thing you can hang onto.

The love of Christ is the same
the same the same the same
same the same the same the s
the same the same the same
same the same the same the s
the same the same the same
same the same the same the s
the same the same the same
same the same the same the
the same the same the same
same the same the same the s
the same the same the same
same the same the same the s
the same the same the same
same the same the same the s
the same the same the same
same the same the same the s
the same the same the same
same the same the same the
the same the same the same
same the same the same the s
the same the same the same
same the same the same the s
the same the same yesterday

the same the same the same
same the same the same the
the same the same the same
same the same the same the
the same the same the same
same the same the same the
the same the same the same
same the same the same the
the same the same the same
same the same the same the
the same the same the same
same the same the same the
the same the same the same
same the same the same the
the same the same the same
same the same the same th
the same the same the same
same the same the same the
the same the same the same
same the same the same the
the same the same the same
same the same the same the
the same the same the same
day, and forever...

GOD IS BEING EDGED OUT OF HIS OWN WORLD

There was a time in the not too distant past when a thunderstorm caused grown men to shudder and feel small. But God is being edged out of His world by science. The more we know about meteorology, the less inclined we are to pray during a thunderstorm. Airplanes now fly above, below, and around them. Satellites reduce them to photographs. What ignominy if a thunderstorm could experience ignominy! Reduced from theophany to nuisance! Certainly, the new can amaze us: a space shuttle, the latest computer game, the softest diaper. Till tomorrow, till the new becomes old, till yesterday's wonder is discarded or taken for granted.

We get so preoccupied with ourselves, the words we speak, the plans and projects we conceive, that we become immune to the glory of creation. We barely notice the cloud passing over the moon or the dewdrops clinging to the rose petals. The ice on the pond comes and goes. The wild blackberries ripen and wither. The blackbird nests outside our bedroom window, but we don't see her. We avoid the cold and the heat. We refrigerate ourselves in summer and entomb ourselves in plastic in winter. We rake up every leaf as fast as it falls.

Our world is saturated with grace, and the lurking presence of God is revealed not only in spirit but in matter—in a deer leaping across a meadow, in the flight of an eagle, in fire and water, in a rainbow after a summer storm, in a gentle doe streaking through a forest, in Beethoven's Ninth Symphony, in a child licking a chocolate ice cream cone, in a woman with windblown hair. God intended for us to discover His loving presence in the world around us.

For several centuries the Celtic church of Ireland was spared the Greek dualism of matter and spirit. They regarded the world with the clear vision of faith. When a young Celtic monk saw his cat catch a salmon swimming in shallow water, he cried, "The power of the Lord is

in the paw of the cat." The Celtic chronicles tell of the wandering sailor monks of the Atlantic, seeing the angels of God and hearing their song as they rose and fell over the western islands. To the scientific person they were only gulls and gannets, puffins, cormorants and kittiwakes. But the monks lived in a world in which everything was a word of God to them, in which the love of God was manifest to anyone with the least creative imagination. How else, they wondered, would God speak to them? They cherished the Scriptures, but they also cherished God's ongoing revelation in His world of grace. "Nature breaks through the eyes of a cat," they said. For the eyes of faith, every created thing manifests the grace and providence of Abba. †

Several years before his death, a remarkable rabbi, Abraham Joshua Heschel, suffered a near-fatal heart attack. His closest male friend was at his bedside. Heschel was so weak he was only able to whisper. "Sam," he said, "I feel only gratitude for my life, for every moment I have lived. I am ready to go. I have seen so many miracles during my lifetime." The old rabbi was exhausted by his effort to speak. After a long pause, he said, "Never once in my life did I ask God for success or wisdom or power or fame. I asked for wonder, and He gave it to me."

I asked for wonder, and He gave it to me. A Philistine will stand before a Claude Monet painting and pick his nose; a person filled with wonder will stand there fighting back the tears.

A story is told about Fiorello LaGuardia, who, when he was mayor of New York City during the worst days of the Great Depression and all of World War II, was called "the Little Flower" by adoring New Yorkers because he was only five foot four and always wore a carnation in his lapel. He was a colorful character who used to ride the New York City fire trucks, raid speakeasies with the police department, take entire orphanages to baseball games, and whenever the New York newspapers were on strike, he would go on the radio and read the Sunday funnies to the kids.

One bitterly cold night in January of 1935, the mayor turned up at a night court that served the poorest ward of the city. LaGuardia dismissed the judge for the evening and took over the bench himself. Within a few minutes, a tattered old woman was brought before him, charged with stealing a loaf of bread. She told LaGuardia that her daughter's husband had deserted her, her daughter was sick, and her two grandchildren were starving. But the shopkeeper, from whom the bread was stolen, refused to drop the charges. "It's a bad neighborhood, Your Honor," the man told the mayor. "She's got to be punished to teach other people around here a lesson."

LaGuardia sighed. He turned to the woman and said, "I've got to punish you. The law makes no exceptions—ten dollars or ten days in jail." But even as he pronounced the sentence, the mayor was already reaching into his pocket. He extracted a bill and tossed it into his famous sombrero, saying, "Here is the ten dollar fine, which I now remit; and furthermore I am going to fine everyone in this courtroom fifty cents for living in a town where a person has to steal bread so that her grandchildren can eat. Mr. Bailiff, collect the fines and give them to the defendant."

So the following day the New York City newspapers reported that $47.50 was turned over to a bewildered old lady who had stolen a loaf of bread to feed her starving grandchildren, fifty cents of that amount being contributed by the red-faced grocery store owner, while some seventy petty criminals, people with traffic violations, and New York City policemen, each of whom had just paid fifty cents for the privilege of doing so, gave the mayor a standing ovation.

What an extraordinary moment of grace for everyone present in that courtroom! The grace of God operates at a profound level in the life of a loving person. Oh, that we would recognize God's grace when it comes to us! †

from whom the bread was stolen

Oh, that WE would recognize God's grace when it comes to US!

In the grasp of wonder

The spirituality of wonder knows the world is charged with grace, that while sin and war, disease and death are terribly real, God's loving presence and power in our midst are even more real.

In the grasp of wonder, I am surprised, I'm enraptured. It's Moses before the burning bush "afraid to look at God" (Exodus 3:6). It's Stephen about to be stoned: "I can see...the Son of man standing at the right hand of God" (Acts 7:56). It's Michelangelo striking his sculptured Moses and commanding him, "Speak!" It's Ignatius of Loyola in ecstasy as he eyes the sky at night, Teresa of Avila ravished by a rose. It's doubting Thomas discovering his God in the wounds of Jesus, Mother Teresa spying the face of Christ in the tortured poor. It's America thrilling to footsteps on the moon, a child casting his kite to the wind. It's a mother looking with love at her newborn infant. It's the wonder of a first kiss.

Let us ask God for the gift He gave to an unforgettable rabbi, Joshua Abraham Heschel:

"Dear Lord, grant me the grace of wonder. Surprise me, amaze me, awe me in every crevice of Your universe. Delight me to see how Your Christ plays in ten thousand places, lovely in limbs, and lovely in eyes not His, to the Father through the features of men's faces. Each day enrapture me with Your marvelous things without number. I do not ask to see the reason for it all; I ask only to share the wonder of it all." †

Counterfeit grace is as commonplace as fake furs, phony antiques, paste jewelry, and saw-dust hot dogs. The tempation of the age is to look good without being good.

"WHITE LIES" were criminal offenses, we would all be in jail by nightfall.

World of Shadows

The Evil One is the great illusionist. He varnishes the truth and encourages dishonesty. "If we say, '**We have no sin**,' we are deceiving ourselves, and the truth has no place in us" (1 John 1:8). Satan prompts us to give importance to what has no importance. He clothes trivia with glitter and seduces us away from what is real. He causes us to live in a world of delusion, unreality, and shadows.

The noonday devil of the Christian life is the temptation to lose the inner self while preserving the shell of edifying behavior. Suddenly I discover that I am ministering to AIDS victims to enhance my résumé.

In the most humiliating sense of the word, I have become a legalist. I have fallen victim to what T. S. Eliot calls the greatest sin: to do the right thing for the wrong reason.

"Beware of the scribes...these are the men who devour the property of widows and for show offer long prayers" (Mark 12:38-40).

The letter of James counsels us to confess our sins to one another (James 5:16). This salutary practice aims to guide us in accepting ownership of our ragamuffin status. But as Dietrich Bonhoeffer noted: He who is alone with his sins is utterly alone. It may be that Christians, notwithstanding corporate worship, common prayer, and all their fellowship in service, may still be left to their loneliness. The final breakthrough to fellowship does not occur because, though they have fellowship with one another as believers and as devout people, they do not have fellowship as the undevout, as sinners. The pious fellowship permits no one to be a sinner. So everyone must conceal his sin from himself and from their fellowship. **We dare not be sinners**. Many Christians are unthinkably horrified when a real sinner is suddenly discovered among the righteous. So we remain alone with our sin, living in lies and hypocrisy. The fact is that we are sinners!

The appeal of paste jewelry and sawdust hot dogs is powerful. A small investment in apparent propriety and good deeds yields the rewards of the faith community—adulation and praise. Coupled with a charismatic personality and an attractive appearance, hypocrisy can earn a $640,000 apartment at Trump Towers, a $90,000 diamond ring from Tiffany's, and frequent flights to Europe. †

Relief comes from rigorous honesty with ourselves.

Honesty...is always unpleasant, and usually painful, and that is why I am not very good at it. But to stand in the truth before God and one another has a unique reward. It is the reward which a sense of reality always brings: I know something extremely precious. I am in touch with myself as I am. My tendency to play the pseudo-messiah is torpedoed.

To the extent that I reject my ragamuffin identity, I turn away from God, the community, and myself. I become a man obsessed by illusion, a man of false power and fearful weakness, unable to think, act, or love.

Gerald May, a Christian psychiatrist in Washington DC, writes: "Honesty before God requires the most fundamental risk of faith we can take: the risk that God is good, that **God does love us unconditionally**. It is in taking this risk that we rediscover our dignity. To bring the truth of ourselves, just as we are, to God, just as God is, is the most dignified thing we can do in this life." ✝

THE MOST

GNIFIED THING WE CAN DO

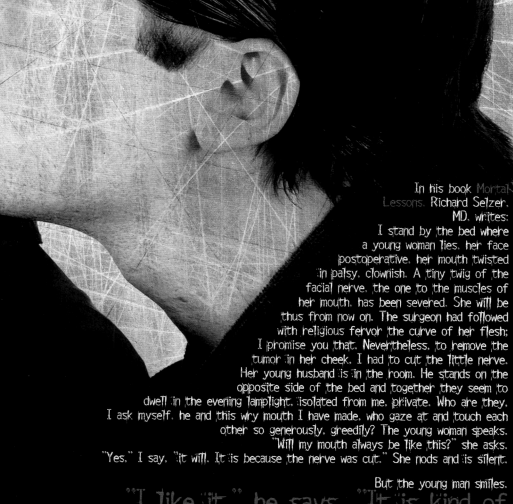

In his book Mortal Lessons, Richard Selzer, MD, writes:

I stand by the bed where a young woman lies, her face postoperative, her mouth twisted in palsy, clownish. A tiny twig of the facial nerve, the one to the muscles of her mouth, has been severed. She will be thus from now on. The surgeon had followed with religious fervor the curve of her flesh; I promise you that. Nevertheless, to remove the tumor in her cheek, I had to cut the little nerve. Her young husband is in the room. He stands on the opposite side of the bed and together they seem to dwell in the evening lamplight, isolated from me, private. Who are they, I ask myself, he and this wry mouth I have made, who gaze at and touch each other so generously, greedily? The young woman speaks. "Will my mouth always be like this?" she asks.

"Yes," I say, "it will. It is because the nerve was cut." She nods and is silent.

But the young man smiles. "I like it," he says. "It is kind of cute."

All at once I know who he is. I understand and I lower my gaze. One is not bold in an encounter with a god. Unmindful, he bends to kiss her crooked mouth and I am so close I can see how he twists his own lips to accommodate to hers, to

In 1963 a friend gave me an expensive crucifix.
A French artist had carved in wood, carved very delicately,
the hands of Jesus on the cross. On Good Friday the
Roman artists carved—O God, how they carved!—our brother
Jesus with no trouble at all. No art was needed to bang in
the nails with hammers, no red lead to make real blood gush
from His hands, feet, and side. His mouth was contorted
and His lips twisted simply by hoisting Him up on the
crossbeam. We have so theologized the passion and death
of this sacred man that we no longer see the slow
unraveling of His tissue, the spread of
gangrene, His raging thirst.

I stroll down Royal Street in the French Quarter in New Orleans. Adjacent to the infamous Bourbon Street with its jazz emporiums, T-shirt stores, and sex boutiques, Royal is studded with antique shops. "Come look at this," says the antique dealer. "The Venus costs more, but this ivory

And the more we reproduce

Christ crucified is beautiful in its own way, especially against a black velvet backdrop." And the more we reproduce Him, the more we forget about Him and the agony of His third hour. We turn Him into gold, silver, ivory, marble, or whatever to free ourselves from His agony and death as a man.

"For our sake God made the sinless one into sin, so that in him we might become the goodness of God." (2 Corinthians 5:21)

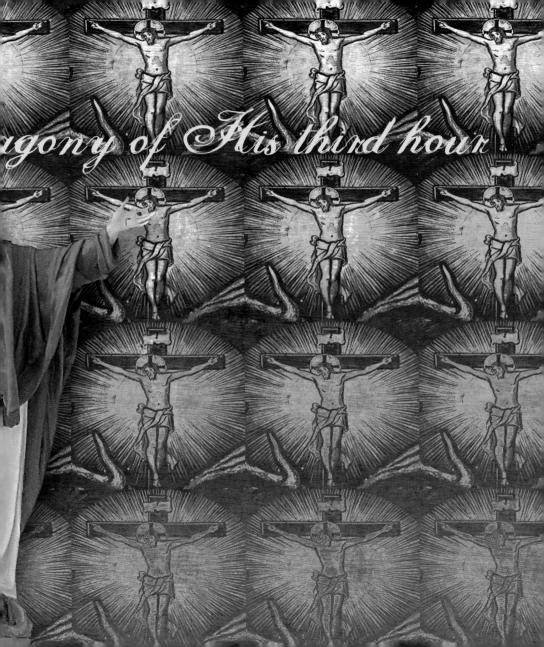

agony of His third hour

Jesus
is God

Jesus has journeyed to the far reaches of loneliness. In His broken body He has carried your sins and mine, every separation and loss, every heart broken, every wound of the spirit that refuses to close, all the riven experiences of men, women, and children across the bands of time.

Jesus is God. You and I were fashioned from the clay of the earth and the kiss of His mouth.

What shall we say to such an outpouring of love? How shall we respond?

First, the love of Christ and His gospel of grace calls for a personal, free, and unconventional decision. To respond is to acknowledge that the other has taken the initiative and issued the invitation. The other's overture has made a response necessary.

However, the other is not some itinerant salesperson at the door peddling bric-a-brac. It is Christ offering the opportunity of a lifetime: "I have come into the world as light, to prevent anyone who believes in me from staying in the dark any more" (John 12:46). ✝

THERE IS AN EXTRAORDINARY POWER
IN STORYTELLING THAT STIRS THE
IMAGINATION AND MAKES AN INDELIBLE
IMPRESSION ON THE MIND. JESUS EMPLOYS
A SET OF STORIES, KNOWN AS THE
"CRISIS" PARABLES, TO ISSUE A WARNING,
A SUMMONS TO REPENTANCE, BECAUSE OF
THE LATENESS OF THE HOUR. JESUS SAYS,
"A TIDAL WAVE IS APPROACHING AND YOU
ARE LOLLYGAGGING ON THE PATIO HAVING
A PARTY." OR AS JOACHIM JEREMIAS PUTS
IT, "YOU ARE FEASTING AND DANCING—ON
THE VOLCANO WHICH MAY ERUPT AT
ANY MOMENT." THE IMPENDING CRISIS
PRECLUDES PROCRASTINATION: "STAY
AWAKE, BECAUSE YOU DO NOT KNOW WHEN
THE MASTER OF THE HOUSE IS COMING,
EVENING, MIDNIGHT, COCKCROW, DAWN; IF
HE COMES UNEXPECTEDLY, HE MUST NOT
FIND YOU ASLEEP. AND WHAT I SAY TO YOU,
I SAY TO ALL: 'STAY AWAKE!'"

What shall we say to such an outpouring of love? Most of us postpone a decision hoping that Jesus will get weary of waiting and the inner voice of Truth will get laryngitis. Thus, the summons of the crisis parables remains suspended in a state of anxiety, so long as we opt neither for nor against the new dimension of living open to us. Our indecision creates more problems than it solves. Indecision means we stop growing for an indeterminate length of time; we get stuck. With the paralysis of analysis, the human spirit begins to shrivel. The conscious awareness of our resistance to grace and the refusal to allow God's love to make us who we really are brings a sense of oppression. Our lives become fragmented, inconsistent, lacking in harmony and out of sync. The worm turns. The felt security of staying in a familiar place vanishes. We are caught between a rock and hard place. How do we resolve this conundrum?

We don't.

We cannot will ourselves to accept grace. There are no magic words, preset formulas, or esoteric rites of passage. Only Jesus Christ sets us free from indecision. The Scriptures offer no other basis for conversion than the personal magnetism of the Master.

For those who feel their lives are a grave disappointment to God, it requires enormous trust and reckless, raging confidence to accept that the love of Christ knows no shadow of alteration or change. When Jesus said, **"Come to me, all you who labor and are heavy burdened,"** He assumed we would grow weary, discouraged, and disheartened along the way.

"For the high priest we have is not incapable of feeling our weaknesses with us, but has been put to the test in exactly the same way as ourselves, apart from sin. Let us, then, have no fear in approaching the throne of grace to receive mercy and to find grace when we are in need of help" (Hebrews 4:15-16). †

How do we resolve this?

When we wallow in guilt, remorse, and shame over real or imagined sins of the past, we are disdaining God's gift of grace. Preoccupation with self is always a major component of unhealthy guilt and recrimination. It stirs our emotions, churning in self-destructive ways, closes us in upon the mighty citadel of self, leads to depression and despair, and preempts the presence of a compassionate God. The language of unhealthy guilt is harsh. It is demanding, abusing, criticizing, rejecting, accusing, blaming, condemning, reproaching, and scolding.

Several years ago in a large city in the far West, rumors spread that a certain Catholic woman was having visions of Jesus. The reports reached the archbishop. He decided to check her out. There is always a fine line between the authentic mystic and the lunatic fringe.

"Is it true, ma'am, that you have visions of Jesus?" asked the cleric.

"Yes," the woman replied simply.

"Well, the next time you have a vision, I want you to ask Jesus to tell you the sins that I confessed in my last confession."

The woman was stunned. "Did I hear you right, bishop? You actually want

me to ask Jesus to tell me the sins of your past?"

"Exactly. Please call me if anything happens."

Ten days later the woman notified her spiritual leader of a recent apparition. "Please come," she said.

Within the hour the archbishop arrived. He trusted eye-to-eye contact. "You just told me on the telephone that you actually had a vision of Jesus. Did you do what I asked?"

"Yes, bishop, I asked Jesus to tell me the sins you confessed in your last confession."

The bishop leaned forward with anticipation. His eyes narrowed.

"What did Jesus say?"

She took his hand and gazed deep into his eyes. "Bishop," she said, "these are His exact words: **I CAN'T REMEMBER**.'" †

IN A LARGE CITY

I can't remember

I can't

remember

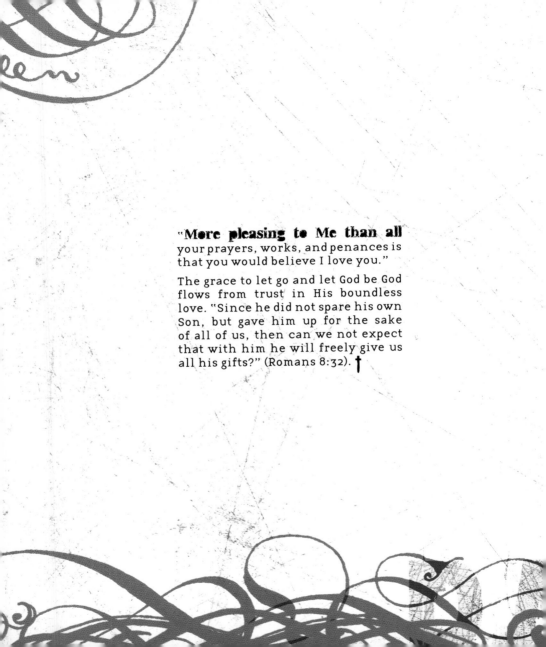

"**More pleasing to Me than all** your prayers, works, and penances is that you would believe I love you."

The grace to let go and let God be God flows from trust in His boundless love. "Since he did not spare his own Son, but gave him up for the sake of all of us, then can we not expect that with him he will freely give us all his gifts?" (Romans 8:32). ✝

"I love you."

I'll catch you

A TWO-STORY HOUSE HAD CAUGHT ON FIRE. THE FAMILY—FATHER, MOTHER, SEVERAL CHILDREN—WERE ON THEIR WAY OUT WHEN THE SMALLEST BOY BECAME TERRIFIED, TORE AWAY FROM HIS MOTHER, RAN BACK UPSTAIRS. SUDDENLY HE APPEARED AT A SMOKE-FILLED WINDOW, CRYING LIKE CRAZY. HIS FATHER, OUTSIDE, SHOUTED, "JUMP, SON, JUMP! I'LL CATCH YOU." THE BOY CRIED, "BUT, DADDY, I CAN'T SEE YOU." "I KNOW," HIS FATHER CALLED, "I KNOW. BUT I CAN SEE YOU."

I wish for you the awakening I experienced many years ago during a spiritual sojourn in the Saragosa Desert in Spain. One night I went to the chapel to pray. The world was asleep, but my heart was awake to the Lord and I stood at the crucifix for a long time. Then in faith, I heard Jesus Christ say, "For love of you, I left my Father's side and I came to you, who ran from Me, who fled Me, who did not want to hear My name. For love of you, I was covered with spit and punched and beaten and fixed to the wood of the cross.

I figuratively saw blood streaming from every wound and pore in Christ's body. And I heard the cry of His blood, "THIS ISN'T A JOKE. It is not a laughing matter to Me that I have loved you. The longer I looked, the more I realized that no man has ever loved me and no woman could ever love me as He does.

THIS ISN

T A JOKE

I went out into the darkness and shouted into the night, "JESUS, ARE YOU CRAZY? ARE YOU OUT OF YOUR MIND TO HAVE LOVED ME SO MUCH?"

The day I joined the order, an old Franciscan told me, "Once you come to experience the love of Jesus Christ, nothing else in the world will seem beautiful or desirable." That night I learned first-hand what he meant.

The nature of God's love for us is outrageous. Why doesn't this God of ours display some taste and discretion in dealing with us? Why doesn't He show more restraint? To be blunt about it, couldn't God arrange to have a little more dignity? Wow!

No, the love of our God isn't dignified at all, and apparently that's the way He expects our love to be for others.

Jesus, are You crazy?

In the final analysis, the real challenge of Christian growth is the challenge of personal responsibility. The Spirit of Jesus calls out a second time: Are you going to take charge of your life today? Are you going to be responsible for what you do? Are you going to believe? Perhaps we are all in the position of the man in Morton Kelsey's story who came to the edge of an abyss. As he stood there, wondering what to do next, he was amazed to discover a tightrope stretched across the abyss. And slowly, surely, across the rope came an acrobat pushing before him a wheelbarrow with another performer in it. When they finally reached the safety of solid ground, the acrobat smiled at the man's amazement. "Don't you think I can do it again?" he asked. And the man replied, "Why yes, I certainly believe you can."

The acrobat put his question again, and when the answer was the same, he pointed to the wheelbarrow and said, "Good! Then get in and I will take you across." What did the traveler do? This is just the question

I will

we have to ask ourselves about Jesus Christ. Do we state our belief in Him in no uncertain terms, even in finely articulated creeds, and then refuse to get into the wheelbarrow? What we do about the lordship of Jesus is a better indication of our faith than what we think.

———— Special E

GRATUITOUS

The Gospel of Gra
Forgiveness Prece

The sinner is accepted before he pleads for mercy. It is already granted. He need only receive it. Total amnesty. Gratuitous pardon.

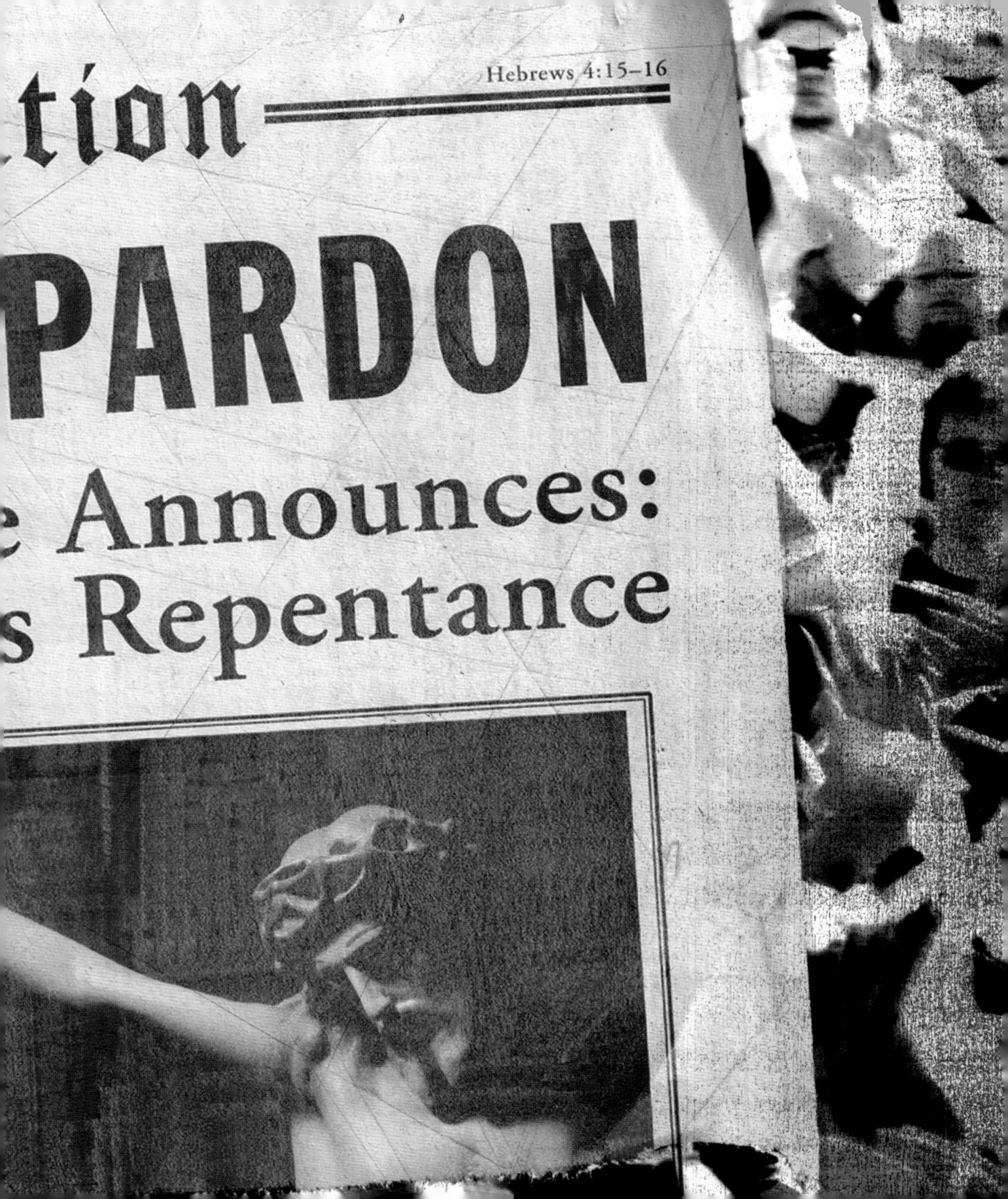

tion
Hebrews 4:15–16
PARDON
e Announces:
s Repentance

When the prodigal son limped home from his lengthy binge of waste and wandering, boozing and womanizing, his motives were mixed at best. He said to himself, "How many of my father's hired men have all the food they want and more, and here am I dying of hunger! I will leave this place and go to my father" (Luke 15:17–18). The ragamuffin stomach was not churning with compunction because he had broken his father's heart. He stumbled home simply to survive. His sojourn in a far country had left him bankrupt. The days of wine and roses had left him dazed and disillusioned. The wine soured and the roses withered. His declaration of independence had reaped an unexpected harvest: not freedom, joy, and new life but bondage, gloom, and a brush with death. His fair-weather friends had shifted their allegiance when his piggy bank emptied. Disenchanted with life, the wastrel weaved his way home, not from a burning desire to see his father, but just to stay alive.

For me, the most touching verse in the entire Bible is the father's response: "While he was still a long way off, his father saw him and was moved with pity. He ran to the boy, clasped him in his arms and kissed him" (Luke 15:20). I am moved that the father didn't cross-examine the boy, bully him, lecture him on ingratitude, or insist on any high motivation. He was so overjoyed at the sight of his son that he ignored all the canons of prudence and parental discretion and simply welcomed him home. The father took him back just as he was.

What a word of encouragement, consolation, and comfort! We don't have to sift our hearts and analyze our intentions before returning home. Abba just wants us to show up. We don't have to tarry at the tavern until purity of heart arrives. We don't have to be shredded with sorrow or crushed with contrition. We don't have to be perfect or even very good before God will accept us. We don't have to wallow in guilt, shame, remorse, and self-condemnation. Even if we still nurse a secret nostalgia for the far country, **Abba falls on our neck and kisses us**.

On the last day, when we arrive at the Great Cabin in the Sky, many of us will be bloodied, battered, bruised, and limping. But by God and by Christ, there will be a light in the window and a **"Welcome Home"**

BRENNAN MANNING

is a Korean War veteran and former Franciscan priest now residing in New Orleans, Louisiana. While he has held various academic and ministry positions at colleges and universities, one of Brennan's most pivotal moments came during a retreat in an isolated cave, where he was powerfully convicted by the revelation of God's love in the crucified Christ. Brennan is the bestselling author of more than a dozen books, including *The Signature of Jesus* and *Abba's Child.* Manning travels widely and continues to write and preach, sharing the good news of God's unconditional love in Jesus Christ.

CHARLES BROCK

Charles Brock is a graphic designer and art director for The DesignWorks Group in Sisters, Oregon. His love for books and reading propelled him into the book design business eight years ago, after graduating from Oklahoma State University/ Okmulgee. His works have been featured in *Communication Arts.* He enjoys spending his spare time with his wife, Kimberly, and pursuing his interests in photography.

Cover imagery: www.photos.com, www.istockphoto.com

Interior imagery: www.istockphoto.com, www.photos.com, www.imageafter.com, Photodisc, Digital Stock, Image Club Graphics, Photospin, www.brockimages.com, Craig Morton

Illustrations on pages 36-37 & 164-165 by Aaron Whisner, www.aaronwhisner.com

Back cover photo by Steve Gardner, www.pixelworksstudio.net

Nose pick model: Tim Green

Creative Development: David Kopp

SOURCES

Afraid to dance—Eugene O'Neill, *The Great God Brown* (1926).

Reformation—Jaroslav Pelikan, *Jesus Through the Centuries: His Place in the History of Culture* (New Haven, CT: Yale University Press, 1985), 158.

Accepted—Paul Tillich, *The Shaking of the Foundations* (New York: Scribner's, 1948), 161-62.

Lowest and the least—Albert Nolan, *Jesus Before Christianity* (Maryknoll, NY: Orbis Books, 1978), 56.

Converted from the bad news—Donald P. Gray, *Jesus: The Way to Freedom* (Winona, MN: St. Mary's College, 1979), 33, 19.

Random sampling—Marcus S. Borg, *Jesus, A New Vision: Spirit, Culture, and the Life of Discipleship* (New York: Harper & Row, 1987), 35.

God is being edged out—Sean Caulfield, *The God of Ordinary People* (Kansas City, MO: Sheed and Ward, 1988), 50.

>From whom the bread was stolen—James N. McCutcheon, "The Righteous and the Good," in *Best Sermons* (San Francisco: Harper & Row, 1988), 238-39.

Kind of cute—Richard Selzer, MD, *Mortal Lessons: Notes on the Art of Surgery* (New York: Simon and Shuster, 1978), 45-46.

Stay awake—Joachim Jeremias, *The Parables of Jesus* (New York: Charles Scribner's Sons, 1970), 72.